The Gesäuse Rapids, a ten-mile-long gorge where the River Enns breaks through the Ennstal Alps.

Marion Schmid

Austria in picture

Helmut Schmid Verlag
Salzburg-Regensburg

Lithograph reproductions: Ludwig, Zell am See
Text: Doris Esser, Salzburg
Translation: Adrian Towersey, B.A.
Preparation: Peter Stemmle (technical adviser)
Paper: Euroart 170 gr der PWA-G
Production: Schmid-Verlag, Salzburg
ISBN 3-900 284-02-4

FOREWORD

Every year millions of visitors from all parts of the world flood into Austria, the "Red-White-and-Red Republic", whose happy fate it is to live from other people coming to look at and admire it. Austria is not yet a country in which one has to go to the cinema in order to marvel at nature – here one has it on one's own doorstep.

The Austrian greatly values the jewel that he possesses, and sometimes his love for his native land becomes so passionate that the attachment can be highly infectious. The by no means few Germans, Scandinavians and Americans who have settled for good in this country after getting to know it for the first time are telling evidence that you cannot easily get rid of the Austria bug that persists between the Alps and Lake Neusiedl.

Who is it that the esteemed guest meets when he has crossed the frontiers of this small Central European state? Should his route first lead to Vienna, he will probably get the feeling he is still in the powerful monarchy of the days when Czechs, Slovaks, Galicians, Hungarians and Slavs were under the rule of a single throne, that of the Habsburgs. Not only the names in the Vienna telephone directory are a reminder of the many nations that went to make up Austria in the past.

In addition to the Viennese, the Styrians, in particular the natives of Graz, are proud of their imperial past. But that should not obscure the fact that Graz is also the centre for a courageous, at times even rebellious, avant-garde theatre and that it is therefore an intellectual workshop for modern times in a cosmopolitan setting.

Turning to the native of Upper Austria, one finds that he has put on his seven-league boots to make up the lost ground towards so-called economic prosperity. However, he would not be an Austrian if he did not like to think back in pride to the sons who have carried the fame of this federal state out into the world: the great composer Anton Bruckner and the poet Adalbert Stifter with his subtle expression of feeling.

The Austrian is said to be easy-going, affable and partial to a sing-song. But Whoever takes this to mean that life for the Austrian is one long round of celebrating and making merry is well wide of the mark. Deep inside, the Austrian is not at all happy with his fate and he likes to flirt with melancholy. Anyone who has had first-hand experience of the Heurige (drinking the new wine) has also got close to the "Viennese soul". A few drops of soulfulness mixed together with some from the heart and stirred up with a little weltschmerz, all washed down in a few glasses of wine to the strains of those violin virtuosos known as Schrammeln, who sound as though they are wailing to the whole world, and the whole thing degenerates into a mournfulness that can only be compared to the sort of depression that might seize one on a rainy day in Montmartre.

Everyone cultivates his melancholy in a different way. The Carinthian sings his sad songs, which pluck at the listener's heartstrings in such a way that tears immediately come to his eyes. The sensible inhabitant of Vorarlberg plunges into his work and as soon as he has achieved some sort of professional success his depression disappears into thin air. The Tyrolean, with both feet firmly on the ground, is never much troubled by weltschmerz. But perhaps the great number of churches freely offering solace from many hilltops have something to do with that. In any case, they are the reason why this part of Austria is called the "Holy Land of Tyrol". The people from Lower Austria and the Burgenland are the perfect hosts and would suppress any sadness right from the start. The Lower Austrian, who sees the Wachau and the Weinviertel ("Wine District") as part of himself, and the inhabitant of the Burgenland, who has an idylllic corner of Paradise to offer with his thatched roofs, draw-wells, storks and windmills, are delighted at the fact that most of their guests come from their own country.

The inhabitant of "Mozart's City" is apparently immune to melancholy. Those who are not natives of the city jokingly claim that in Salzburg from now on they only cross off the days on which the Festival does not take place. And Salzburg indeed seems to be one long festival of music, the year beginning with the Mozart Week dedicated to the local genius, continuing with the Easter, Whitsun and Summer Festivals, and closing with the Autumn Festival of Culture and the choral concerts in Advent.

To many, Austria appears to be a haven of bliss, or even a paradise-on-earth. Here everything still seems to be so wholesome, friendly and full of go. Even the Austrian business world can claim that the darkest clouds on the economic horizon did not gather to discharge their load here, even though a third of the population earn their living in not exactly stable branches of industry like textiles, mechanical engineering, steel production, the iron industry and electronics, to mention just a few. Basically, the Austrian is equipped with a marked optimism that helps him to get through the worst of times and that protects him from any greater misfortune.

And what is the slogan that travel promoters in Carinthia have thought up? "A holiday in Carinthia is a holiday amongst friends." Let this welcoming greeting be said of the whole of Austria, a country in which hospitality is cultivated not only for the purpose of attracting foreign currency.

2

Anyone who thinks of Vorarlberg probably has the Arlberg Mountain in mind, which gives this most westerly federal state its name.

The winter ski runs like those at St. Christoph (left) are some of the finest in Austria.

The Montafon with its "Three Spires", in the picture on the right, is the most southerly valley in Vorarlberg.

From Lake Constance up to the Silvretta the scenery of Vorarlberg shows great variety. The Grosswalsertal is one of the most beautiful mountain valleys in this federal state. In the picture above left: the village of Blons.

The massive Schattenburg dominates the little "school town" of Feldkirch, the ancient seat of the Montforts.

Lake Constance and the Bregenz Festival belong together in people's minds. The most popular operettas are performed on the largest stage erected over water in Europe.

Players of the alpenhorn show their respect for age-old melodies by cultivating them even today.

Comfortable pleasure boats with panorama decks carry passengers across the great lake, where the borders of three countries meet.

On festive occasions the inhabitants of Vorarlberg like to wear their local costume (right).

The Valley of the Tux has preserved its old farms like a precious hoard – fine old farmhouses, built entirely of wood, like this one on the way to the summer skiing area at Hintertux.

Mayrhofen in the Ziller Valley is the starting point for many a climbing tour to the towering peaks, or walking tours over luscious mountain meadows and to lakes where one can bathe in water as clear as glass. All of these excursions include Tyrolean hospitality during a pleasant stop at a wayside inn.

HOTEL A

In folk-songs people often like to sing about Innsbruck on the "Green Inn". The capital of Tyrol, founded in 1180 by the Counts of Andechs, is set in magnificent mountain scenery. Maria-Theresien-Strasse (above left) and the "Golden Roof" are real musts on any visit to Innsbruck. The former Imperial Palace is one of the most imposing buildings in the city. It was built in the late Viennese rococo style. The dress worn by the women in the Valley of the Oetz is an especial gem amongst peasant costumes.

Tyrol, known as the "Holy Land" on account of the innumerable churches that send down solace from their hilltops, has combined the old and the new in a fortunate manner. Without a doubt Tyrol's national sport is skiing, but the young sport of hang gliding also enjoys considerable popularity.

Above left: Kitzbühel, looking towards the Wilder Kaiser Mountains. Above right: A view of the Walder Alm mountain pastures. Below left: Decorative painting on the facade of an inn at Oetz.

The "Mint Tower" in Solbad Hall before the gates of Innsbruck cannot fail to catch one's eye and is a landmark in the town.

The Tyroleans say that whoever goes up into the mountains comes back with his heart lightened. In Eastern Tyrol, which enjoys especially strong sunshine for long hours, there is the Innergschloess with the Grossvenediger Mountain.

The "Zemm Power Plant" is a reservoir high up in the mountains belonging to the Tauern power station and, like the Salzburg power plant at Kaprun, is a top tourist attraction.

Carinthia with its magnificent lakeland scenery is not only a paradise for keen bathers but also for mountainlovers. Here fascinating landscape – none less than the highest mountain in Austria, the 12,457-foot-high Grossglockner – invites one to walks in the mountains.

For all those who pass through the Tauern Tunnel on the motorail service Carinthia begins in Mallnitz. This spa for mountain air is the starting-point for many walks leading into the Ankogel region, into the Goldberg group of mountains or round the Hochalm peak.

Carinthian hospitality makes one feel at home – and Carinthian specialities like noodles with cheese or fresh doughnuts give one the necessary stamina. There are many romantic spots like the fairytale meadow Bodental in the Karawanken Mountains.

Paracelsus, the famous doctor, spent his youth in Villach, now the second-largest city in Carinthia (above left). Villach was blessed with a gift of nature, medicinal springs, at which people received successful treatment as early as in Roman times.

The instantly recognisable symbol of the city is the dragon. The city was founded in 1181 by nobility from the Rhineland Palatinate, the Spannheimer family. The founder, Duke Bernhard, has been commemorated with a statue in front of the parish church.

Idyllic Maria Saal is built on ground laden with history. The fortified pilgrimage church is the oldest in the land. In Maria Saal there also rings the largest bell in Carinthia, the "Maria Saal Bell" weighing six and a half tons, which was cast from captured Turkish cannons.

Endless sports, games and fun in or on the water are certainly no idle promises in Carinthia. Over 200 lakes are an invitation to idyllic settings, sports and a romantic atmosphere.

The Wörthersee is called the "Côte d'azur of Austria" because of its atmosphere of elegance. Water-skiing took on here when it was still hardly known. In the meantime it has been overtaken by windsurfing.

The adventurous are recommended to try some canoeing on the Lieser near Spital, where sometimes even the experts are stunned.

Above left: In the middle of the Zollfeld near Maria Saal stands the ducal throne from which the Dukes of Carinthia administered justice and bestowed fiefs. The Zollfeld is said to be the heart of Carinthia.

Above right: Hochosterwitz is a picture-book fortress. When the Turkish raids were threatening in the 16th century, Baron George of Khevenhueller had the way leading up to the castle fortified with 14 gates, a feature which is unmatched in the rest of the world.

Overleaf left: The construction of the Grossglockner Alpine Highway is a masterpiece of alpine roadbuilding. Its creator, Franz Wallack, is buried in Salzburg.

Overleaf right: At the foot of the Grossglockner in the midst of picturesque mountains lies Heiligenblut, which possesses one of the most perfect Gothic churches in Carinthia.

Salzburg, Innerer Stein, 1846, oil on canvass, by Friedrich Loos, one of the greatest Austrian landscape painters of the 19th century (1797-1890).

Previous double page: View over the City of Salzburg with the Untersberg Mountain in the background.

People often like to ask when the city is at its most beautiful. The answers they get are as varied as the churches, which easily number fifty.

Some say on a snowy December day during a walk on the Mönchsberg Hill, and go into ecstasies about the domes that have all been capped in white.

Others maintain on a hot summer's day in August when one can seek a romantic retreat beneath the thick foliage of the arboured paths in the Mirabell Gardens while the fountains play in iridescent colours.

Salzburg is like a bright butterfly – dreamy in its narrow lanes, hungry for sun on its roofs flooded with light and a-flutter with joy in its Mirabell and Hellbrunn Parks.

Those keen on social excitement claim that Salzburg is at its most exhilarating during the Festival. At the end of July and through the whole of August Salzburg is to all appearances the centre of the cultural world. The finest evening dresses are paraded up and down outside the Great Festival Hall, and inside the best orchestras in the world play the unforgettable works by the most famous son of this city, Wolfgang Amadeus Mozart. Sometimes on such festive days boards ought really to be put up proclaiming "City closed today on account of overcrowding", and that is when many a native of Salzburg is glad to flee on to the Kapuzinerberg ("Hill of the Capuchins") where – right in the middle of town – roebucks and badgers, squirrels and chamois all have a date to meet up.

It is certainly no coincidence that in particular the Mirabell Gardens were laid out in honour of a beautiful woman. In Salzburg, Cupid's arrows did not even spare a most princely archbishop.

"All around is rocky solitude. The faded blooms of death shiver on the graves that mourn in the dark – yet there is no sorrow in this mourning." Georg Trakl, the great poet-son of this city, dedicated a poem to St. Peter's Cemetery and in it described the magic stillness of that particular God's acre. Michael Haydn is buried here as well as Mozart's sister, Nannerl. – After walking past sheer rockfaces, crosses and graves, the visitor is welcomed back into the city.

"The light that enters through the dome of Salzburg Cathedral illuminates every little corner", wrote the composer Franz Schubert enthusiastically. Anyone approaching the portal of the Cathedral from the Church of the Franciscans is deeply impressed by the dignity that this cathedral radiates. – Above right: the existence of present-day Salzburg is reckoned to date from the arrival of St. Rupert.

Prince Eugene is said to have offered 7,000 gulden for this horse statue, but to no avail: the remarkable piece of sculpture remained in Salzburg, and the inhabitants of the city have become deeply attached to the rearing horse.

People flock from all four corners of the world to Mozart's birthplace in the heart of the city. Many of them feel they can still hear the strains of his "Jupiter Symphony", a serenade or a divertimento, the "Magic Flute" or "Figaro". The "infant wonder" first composed at the age of five. Wolfgang Amadeus first saw the light of day on the third floor of house number 9, Getreidegasse, in 1756; many different places in the city were the scenes of his activities: the Cathedral, the Residence, the Robinghof, St. Peter's and Trinity Churches. The bright star in Salzburg's heaven of music still shines as constantly and brilliantly today.

Two things marked Mozart's childhood: the love of acting and imitating and his love of his father, Leopold Mozart. When his father was once holding the score of a piano concerto by the four-year-old boy, two tears of pride and admiration rolled from his eyes.

In spite of his father's uncompromising severity, Mozart was full of affection for him. Every evening he kissed the tip of his papa's nose and vowed that he would always keep him with him in a bell-jar.

Mozart is present in Salzburg at all times and in all places, and there are days when the city is literally submerged in the symphonies of the great composer. The water patters incessantly in the extravagant numbers of fountains as if it, too, wished to show its everlasting veneration for the local genius in whose honour St. Michael's Square was renamed Mozart Square. On that occasion in 1841 a memorial to him was erected there.

The Salzburg Festival began in 1920 with a performance of Hofmannstahl's "Everyman" before the portal to the Cathedral Square. It is now attended by theatrelovers from over seventy countries every year in July and August. The Great Festival Hall can accomodate an audience of 2,170. – With a resplendent performance of Richard Strauss's "Rosenkavalier", Herbert von Karajan inaugurated the Great Festival Hall in his home town in 1960. Anneliese Rothenberger took the part of "Sophie" and Sena Jurinac that of "Octavian".

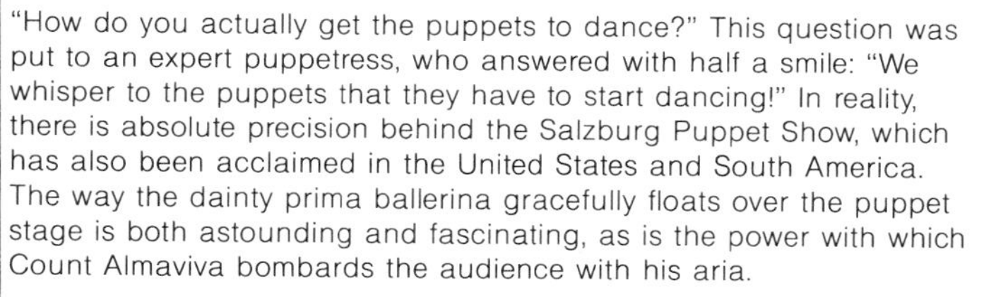

"How do you actually get the puppets to dance?" This question was put to an expert puppetress, who answered with half a smile: "We whisper to the puppets that they have to start dancing!" In reality, there is absolute precision behind the Salzburg Puppet Show, which has also been acclaimed in the United States and South America. The way the dainty prima ballerina gracefully floats over the puppet stage is both astounding and fascinating, as is the power with which Count Almaviva bombards the audience with his aria.

Anyone who loves music feels at home in Salzburg. Concerts of chamber music can be heard here throughout the year. One stumbles upon gems from the past in all corners of Salzburg: the finest late Gothic tiled stove in Austria is to be found in the ornate "Golden Room" in the fortress of Hohensalzburg.
This painting, a portrait of Baroness Waldberg, is by a famous son of this city: Hans Makart, the great 19th-century artist, born in Salzburg in 1840. He was responsible for reviving the baroque heritage of Salzburg and Austria.

The fiacres – horse-drawn carriages – are to Salzburg what the gondolas are to Venice. Thousands of visitors use a two-horse-powered vehicle to get to know the city. – A speciality that melts on the tongue is the "Salzburger Nockerl", a delicious dessert made from eggs and sugar. – Millions of people have already made the obligatory visit to the famous Getreidegasse ("Corn Lane").

Denkstein
Fritsch
Mozart Drogerie
Hotel Goldener Hirsch
OTTO SPORER
SPIRITUOSEN
PHOTO

This fine view of the Hohensalzburg Fortress from the Mirabell Gardens is probably the favourite motif for photographers in Salzburg. – Unicorns, Bacchus, Cronos, Jupiter, Ceres and Diana are just as much part of the Mirabell Gardens as the profoundly ugly dwarves, 13 in number, which are unmatched anywhere else. – The marble staircase in the Mirabell Palace that leads up to the most beautiful and opulent registry office in the world. The baroque angels, created by the baroque sculptor Georg Raphael Donner, are said to bring the newly-weds great good fortune.

Life in the Mirabell Palace is supposed to have been a bright fairy tale – but it was not without its dark side with threatening storm clouds; for, as Erwin Reinalter wrote in his novel "Mirabell", "the world begrudges the individual any undimmed feelings. People saw that the two (Wolf Dietrich and his wife Salome Alt) were reaching out for a joy to which they abandoned themselves in a delirious oblivion of passion; yet it was a sinful joy, since this man should never have been allowed to love; his status forbade him to calm his stormy heart in partnership with a woman."

And historians have passed this judgement on Wolf Dietrich von Raitenau, who at the early age of 28 was created archbishop: "He was a man of excellent intellectual capabilities, but restless and with an insatiable desire for innovation. If he had only moderated his urge for joy and observed the principles of his priestly status, without doubt he would have been a great and illustious prince."

His building fever knew no bounds: he bought up 60 burgher's residences and had them torn down. When Salzburg Cathedral was on fire he is reputed to have said, "Let it burn!" This all fitted in admirably with his plan for an "open city".

He who had wanted to make a German Rome out of Salzburg and had given the city its wide squares and open spaces finally ended up a prisoner in that self-same city. But he forgave his opponents, and in 1617, when Wolf Dietrich died a pious death in the fortress of Hohensalzburg at the age of forty-six, he was something like a martyr, almost a saint, to the citizens of Salzburg.

Wolf Dietrich ordered the Residence to be built in Salzburg as well as Altenau Palace, which was renamed Mirabell by his successor, Markus Sittikus.

While searching for a site on which to build a hunting lodge, Dietrich's successor Markus Sittikus came upon the charming area of Hellbrunn. He had not been able to find any attraction in the fortress of Hohensalzburg because of his cousin's imprisonment there. This archbishop, who was described as being anything from inaccesible to a gentle cavalier, only ruled for seven years. But in that short time he had Salzburg Cathedral built for the faithful, and for himself the pleasure palace and gardens of Hellbrunn. His master builder, Santino Solari, planned and built the palace as a feast of gaiety in which the water was to play its roguish tricks.

The park is set out in the style of a maze. The ibex, the animal in Markus Sittikus's coat of arms, welcomes the visitor. In the Orpheus Grotto (above right) the beasts listen intently to Orpheus, who longs for Eurydice, and outside the Venus Grotto Cupid with eyes bandaged lets fly his arrows in blind rage. In the Birdsong Grotto can be heard the twittering of water-flutes.

Every year half a million visitors go through the experience of Hellbrunn, and even today Hellbrunn is much like an attractive prima donna who seductively tries to win the favour of the esteemed guest. On two weekends in the summer there are celebrations just like those in the days of Markus Sittikus and in the Hall of Frescoes, the Courtyard of Honour and in the Roman Theatre (centre picture) the looker-on falls under the spell of that infectious hilarity. This is the happy place where the historical and the modern, Art and landscape, Nature and architecture meet.

A statue sculpted in honour of the Empress Elizabeth I.

Not only a posy of spices makes the ideal gift. Dried flowers with all the brightness of a summer meadow may delight one's host just as much.

The Christmas carol "Silent Night, Holy Night", which has since found its way to all continents, was first heard in St. Nicholas's Parish Church in Oberndorf. The local priest, Josef Mohr, had written the words and the teacher Franz Xaver Gruber had composed the music.

With the approach of the Christmas season a crib is set up at many farms in the district of Salzburg. The hand-carved wooden figures representing Joseph, Mary, Baby Jesus and the Three Kings are reminders of Christ's birth. One famous builder of cribs is Xandl Schläffer from Saalfeld, who has produced over 800.

One custom in remembrance of the Three Kings is "Sternsingen", when carol singers in oriental finery go from door to door at Epiphany to give their blessing and wish good luck in the New Year to those living in each house. The star is borne on a long pole and can clearly be seen from a distance.

When the nights are at their longest and the snow lies deepest the "Perchten" are out and about. That is to say young men in strange costumes go through the villages and from farm to farm. The ugly Perchten look intimidating and are supposed to drive away fiends and evil. The beautiful Perchten wear ribbons and other bright decoration and carry escutcheons.

he amusing marmot – the "clown of the mountains", so called because of the way it shuffles long and periodically sits up and begs – lives among alpine clover and meadow parsnip. hreatened species: the alpine ibex and the golden eagle. A favourite with hunters: the apercaillie. The edelweiss, gentian and alpine rose are slowly dying out.

The farms of the Salzburg area are generally imposing, apart from the more modest ones high up in the mountains. Common to them all is the "meal-time steeple", a miniature spire carved out of wood mounted with a bell to call the farmers and their hands in for their meals.

Looking down from Salzburg's home mountain, the Gaisberg ("Goat Mountain") towards the River Salzach, the fortress of Hohensalzburg and in the background the Staufen range.

Even though masses of tourists are constantly streaming to the city itself, there are many parts of the Federal State of Salzburg that are still bright and clean. The view of the Bischofsmütze ("Bishop's Mitre Mountain") looking through the autumnal larch woods certainly cannot have been more beautiful a century ago (picture left).

Old farmhouses have been preserved together with the landscape they are set in as if they had been built to last for ever. Some farmers found life hard and moved away; others continued the work of their forefathers and cherish it still.

One old tradition is the carrying of decorated poles in Lungau, which goes back to a vow made in difficult times. Great swarms of locusts had destroyed the harvest, and so the local inhabitants vowed to prevent a repetition of the catastrophe by carrying 26-foot-high poles decorated with flowers through the village every year. This custom can still be seen in Muhr and Zedernhaus today.

Rathaus
Vom Erzbischof
Johann Jakob Khuen
Belasy erbaut im
Jahre 1570 als
Urbarialhaus

The torrent called the Krimmler Ache is an impressive spectacle of nature. Before it joins the Salzach, it makes a roaring and thundering descent of 1,243 feet. The Krimml Waterfalls are the largest in Austria.

The cattle are driven up to the mountain pastures for the summer and back to their winter quarters in the autumn, just as they were centuries ago. If none of the animals has come to grief while grazing in the mountains, the cows are adorned with especially fine ribbons, garlands and alpine flowers, as seen here by the Chapel of Embach.

This, too, is part of the Salzburger Pinzgau district. The Loferer Steinberge ("Rocky Peaks of Lofer") are not as high as the Grossglockner, Hoher Sonnenblick or Grossvenediger mountains, but they are most impressive all the same.

Picture left: The carrying of Samson is one of the old customs of Lungau. The figure weighing 80 kilos, which is borne by one man alone, is modelled on the biblical hero who was so strong that he could tear a lion apart with his bare hands. This fine Samson in a tunic and a toga does not only move solemnly through the town: if he catches a few pleasant strains of music he will even risk a little dance.

Overleaf: The Grossglockner Alpine Highway; below it, the Kirche in der Au ("Chapel in the Meadow") near Lofer; right, the Bischofsmütze Mountain.

There it lies, gay and sensuous – Lake Wolfgang. "In the Salzkammergut, that's where you can be merry!" It is really no surprise that the Salzkammergut is the home of that celebrated operetta "The White Horse Inn". – The winged altar by Michael Pacher in St. Wolfgang's Church is one of the most valuable pieces of Gothic art. Below right: Hallstein at the foot of the Dachstein Mountain, once the centre of the salt trade and the Hallstatt Civilisation.

The district around Lake Aussee has always been a meeting-place for those seeking to relax in peace and quiet. Between mid-May and mid-June, those who love this gem of a landscape flock to Old Aussee, Aussee Spa and to Lake Grundl; that is when carpets of wild daffodils bloom on the slopes leading down to the lake. People come from near and far to celebrate this occasion at a flower festival. The Aussee District is administered by Styria, but is considered part of the Salzkammergut tourist area.

The provincial capital Linz has not lost its baroque appearance: beautiful facades form a setting for the main Square with its Trinity Column. This is one of the largest and finest city squares in Europe. The Landhaus ("Regional Assembly") dating from the early Renaissance is visited by many sightseers. – Right: the Imperial Villa at Bad Ischl, a present to Francis Joseph and Elizabeth from the Empress's mother.

The poet and nature-lover Adalbert Stifter sang the praises of "his" Upper Austria as often as he could: "You can spend days here meditating, and not a sound will disturb your thoughts as they sink into your soul." Above left: St. Nicola, nestling attractively between wooded hills and the Danube, lies in the Strudengau between Grein and Ybbs.

Grein (above right), a village where mainly bargees lived in the old days, is the heart of the Strudengau. In the town hall off the main square there is the oldest municipal theatre in Austria.

Immediate right: In "Suleika" Johann Wolfgang von Goethe created a memorial in poetry dedicated to the beautiful maiden of Linz. It was Marianne von Willemar of Linz that had attracted his admiration and caused him to put his affection into words.

Far right: The alpine resort of Hinterstoder with its overwhelming backdrop of mountains is the dream of all walkers and sportsmen.

The citizens of Graz feel especially attracted to the familiar Clock Tower which gives them a feeling of being really at home. The city is set in surroundings of gently rolling hills that give full rein to one's fantasy. Here the soul can take to the wing like a bright bird of paradise – at least that is what the people of Graz say, and they ought to know.

Hospitality is written big in Graz: the inns are so cosy that husbands often mistake the local for their own home. Of course the excellent international restaurants also attract lovers of good food; but things start to get really "Graz-like" when heavenly dishes such as Altsteirisches Wurzelfleisch ("Traditional Styrian Boiled Pork") or Erdäpfelstrudel ("Potato Strudel") straight from grandma's cookery book appear on the menu.

Many different styles of architecture come together in Graz. Left: the Landhaus, the most important example of Italian Renaissance building north of the Alps. The neighbouring armoury houses sufficient weapons for an army of 30,000 knights.

Mariazell (right) in the east of Styria has been a place of pilgrimage since the 14th century. The faithful flock to the pilgrimage church – the largest church in this federal state – like masses of art-lovers. The altar with the power to work miracles is the work of Fischer von Erlach.

Below left: The Mur Valley Railway, which belongs to the Styrian State Railways, and is still in use today. At the weekend the diesel locomotive is exchanged for a steam engine which puffs through the countryside spewing out fire.

Below right: Italy provided the prototype for the Kornmesserhaus at Bruck on the Mur. It was built in 1499 on the instructions of Pankraz Kornmess, an ironmonger.

Styria seems to be closer to the sun than the other federal states, and here the spring seems to be more fragrant and charming. The brightness of the sun is also reflected in the local costume of Old Aussee (left). – The industry of Styria is a good advertisement for the whole economy. The Erzberg is the most important opencast iron mine in Central Europe and a vital source of employment for the population of Upper Styria. Tourism is the other pillar of the economy. The impressive mountain scenery of Ramsau (below) attracts visitors from far and near.

Immediate left: For centuries the Riegersberg was a frontier stronghold. It proved to be an insurmountable obstacle to the storming Turks.

_eft: This Klapotetz is a typical feature of :he wine-growing area of Southern Styria where vines producing the famous Schil-:her, a rosé of exceptional quality, thrive.

The Dachstein, one of the majestic mountains of Austria, is a favourite climb for keen mountaineers who want to train. "Green Styria" is an idyllic spot where one does not have to go far to find Nature in all her rich, mellow colours and the wide open spaces.

Peter Rosegger's "Forest Home" at Alpl near Krieglach in Styria was a paradise on earth. The everlasting lustre of that writer of Austrian folk-tales has rubbed off on the land and stamped the people who lived here in such an unspoilt and pious manner. Rosegger died in 1918, shortly before the collapse of the Danube Monarchy.

Archduke Johann is to the Styrians what King Ludwig is to the Bavarians. Styria indeed has reason to be most grateful to the son of the Grand Duke Leopold. He came to the throne after the death of Emperor Joseph II. He improved the living conditions of the population by giving planned assistance to agriculture and trade. His love for a postmaster's daughter, Anna Plochl, even affected national politics, but the population only admired Archduke Johann the more for it.

Below: The glow of evening in Ramsau.

Right: The windmill just outside the wine centre of Retz in Lower Austria, a symbol for the whole region. The main square of Retz is one of the finest market squares in Austria.

The Romans introduced wine into Lower Austria, and the wine even outlived the Romans. What is more, it is the most valuable commodity in many districts. Old wine presses, wooden barrels and steps leading down into ancient cellars bear testimony to a wine culture going back over centuries.

Weissenkirchen (left) is the cradle of the Riesling type of wine. The many picturesque lanes and nooks are evidence of a special mixture of romance and culture, an example of which is the 400-year-old Teisenhoferhof housing the Museum of the Wachau. Below right: Langenlois, where Gothic and baroque styles meet. Especially worthy of mention are the Renaissance residences at the Kornplatz ("Corn Square").

Right: A view of Dürnstein in the Wachau, where King Richard the Lion-Heart was held prisoner in 1193. According to legend, his faithful minstrel Blondel found him and got him released. He was heard playing a melody that had always been the King's favourite tune on his lute. It was not long before the King gave an answer from his dungeon: "Hurry back to England and collect money for my ransom, my dear Blondel!"

The library at the Abbey of Melk is a special treat for all art-lovers: over 80,000 volumes including manuscripts and specimens from the early days of printing are preserved on the shelves there. The paintings on the ceiling, which dominate the whole place, are the work of Paul Troger. The Benedictine Abbey is one of the most impressive baroque buildings there is; it was constructed by the baroque master builder Jakob Prandtauer on a 187-foot-high promontory of rock in the years after 1702. It is a landmark of the Wachau and can be seen from miles away.

Heiligenkreuz with its Cistercian abbey of the same name has been a lively cultural centre since the days of the Babenbergs. Margrave Leopold III founded the abbey and in 1135 construction work was started on the basilica. The stained glass windows coloured by applying the grisaille technique are a real jewel. Highly-gifted musicians such as Franz Schubert and Anton Bruckner have played the powerful organ. Pictured right: Leopold the Holy.

Far right: the 13th-century fortress of Heidenreichstein, for a time in the possession of the Kuenring family, is considered to be the finest moated castle in Austria.

St. Stephen's Cathedral, lovingly nicknamed "Steffl" by the inhabitants of Vienna, who number over a million, is the best-known landmark of the metropolis. The Central Cemetery is one of the sights of Vienna. – St. Virgil's Chapel beneath St. Stephen's Square dates from the early 14th century. – The pulpit in the Cathedral by master sculptor Anton Pilgram. – The Votive Church in the centre of Vienna was built between 1865 and 1879.

SOUVENIR · WÄSCHE
A. FISCHER u. C
COIFFEUR

Left: St. Michael's was formerly the church used by the court. Above: The Parliament, where votes are taken that determine Austria's future. It is the seat of the National and Federal Assemblies. Below: The gorgeous baroque St. Charles' Church.

Vienna is a cultural centre and in addition a pulsating modern city. The City Hall (left) is one of the typical buildings along the Ring Road that all have one thing in common: they are imitations of long-gone styles of architecture. The City Hall is mock Gothic, other buildings mock Renaissance. The Viennese call it an architectural fancy-dress party.

St. Michael's Gate certainly commands awe and respect since it is one of the most impressive buildings in Vienna. The plans for the dome were drawn up by Fischer von Erlach.

Below: The view from the Square of the Heroes looking towards the New Hofburg offers a really majestic scene. This south wing of the "Burg", a city within a city, is an example of the fine neo-Gothic style to be seen along the Ring Road.

"The wages of sin is the Turk!" That was the severe warning that abbot Abraham à Santa Clara gave to his "sinful contemporaries". In 1683 the Turks were before the gates of Vienna for the second time, and if the relieving army under John Sobieski, King of Poland, and Charles of Lorraine had not intervened, things would not have looked very rosy for Vienna.

Rulers who held the fortunes of Austria in their hands: Empress Maria Theresa, Emperor Francis Joseph I and the Empress Elizabeth, affectionately known as "Sissi". When the 23-year-old Maria Theresa was crowned Empress in 1740, there was great unrest in the country and the Empire was threatening to disintegrate. The sovereign showed remarkable courage, tenacity and political skill, especially in her dealings with the arch-enemy Frederick II of Prussia. She gave birth to 16 children. Her actions were always dominated by her heart and her motto was: "A mediocre peace is better than a glorious war."

Emperor Francis Joseph I is remembered by the Austrians as the "Emperor of all the Emperors", not least on account of his long reign of 68 years. When he died in 1916 at the age of 86, the monarchy was nearing its end. Especially the misfortune that the Emperor suffered touched the hearts of the people. His brother Maximilian, Emperor of Mexico, was assassinated; his son Rudolph committed suicide, and his wife Sissi was stabbed to death by a Serbian anarchist.

Below left: The imperial family's vault where Maria Theresa and her husband Francis I found their final rest.

Schönbrunn Palace was Maria Theresa's favourite residence. Here the wedding reception of her son Joseph II and his bride Isabella of Parma took place, and Francis Joseph I enjoyed the happy days of his love for Sissi. Here, too, the monarch died a solitary death as the "hermit of Schönbrunn". – Nowadays the Great Gallery in the palace is the magnificent setting for festive state receptions.

Right: The Fountain of Providence at New Market Square, the work of Georg Raphael Donner, portrays symbolically the rivers of Austria.

Vienna's museums number more than fifty – from the modest Fiakermuseum ("Coach Museum") in the suburbs to the world-famous Museum of Art History. The overwhelming abundance to be found in the latter sets it on a par with the Prado und the Louvre. Its main attractions are paintings by Rubens, Titian, Velazquez and in particular the largest collection in the world of works by Bruegel.

Queen Elizabeth II expressed her fervent admiration for the white thoroughbreds; Jimmy Carter, President of the USA, was deeply impressed. The Spanish Riding School, originally founded by the Habsburgs, is the oldest court riding school in the world. Anyone who has ever seen those Lipizzaners perform a levade, a capriole and a courbette in a demonstration of jumping is unlikely to forget either the brilliantly trained animals or their riders in their riding jackets buttoned up to the collar, their white leather jodhpurs, their two-pointed hats and boots with spurs, all a reminder of the pomp and brilliance of the old Danube Monarchy.

Below: The Hofburg ("Imperial Palace") in Vienna, part of which is occupied by the Spanish Riding School, also houses the vaults with their secular und religious treasures. Here one can admire the magnificent main hall of the National Library. The official residence of the Federal President is situated in the Leopold Wing, where Maria Theresa once had her appartments.

He was the greatest war hero in the first half of the 18th century: Prince Eugene of Savoy, born in Paris in 1663. His motto was "Austria über alles!" The respectful admiration that his soldiers had for him points to his benevolence, which is also expressed in the delightful folk-song "Prince Eugene, the Noble Knight".

Below left: Looking through the wrought-iron gate towards the Belvedere, designed as the summer seat of Prince Eugene of Savoy by Lukas von Hildebrandt, with the Lower Belvedere as a residence and the Upper Belvedere (overleaf) for great receptions and festivities.

The old city centre with its many fine burghers' residences huddles round the Cathedral. – Looking over the roofs with the "Steffel" in the background. – Whoever takes a room at the high-class Hotel Sacher does not "stay" there; he or she "resides". – A favourite occupation of the Viennese is having a cup of coffee and reading the newspaper.

"The situation is hopeless, but not serious," say the Viennese, whose much-discussed character is not always bright und breezy. The best recipe for moodiness is the blissfulness of a good glass of wine. "An outing to a Heuriger (festival or inn where the new wine is drunk) saves a visit to the psychiatrist – because only after seven quarters (quarter-litres of wine) does life become really worth living." And when the violins of a Schrammel quartet strike up soulfully, then the native of Vienna is in his seventh heaven.

Vienna would not be half what it is without the Prater, a dazzlingly colourful fairground. The House of Horrors, the Hall of Mirrors, Looping the Loop and the Great Wheel help everyone to forget their troubles.

Vienna is a first-class cultural centre. Anyone who has played a role on the stage of the Burgtheater ("Court Theatre") may be assured of a successful acting career (above). – The Vienna Boys' Choir has become world famous as a result of innumerable concert tours. – The place of remembrance dedicated to the great composer Franz Schubert.

Viennese opera-lovers are proud to say that the Vienna State Opera belongs to the small group of world-class opera houses. – A visit to the Vienna Opera is always a festive occasion. – The hub of the Viennese concert scene is the auditorium of the Musikverein.

Hardly any other city has erected so many statues in memory of its composers: Ludwig van Beethoven, who came to Vienna from Bonn, and Joseph Haydn, who both exercised their talents here.

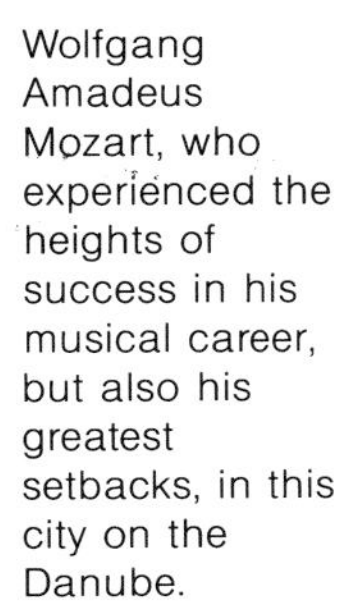

Wolfgang Amadeus Mozart, who experienced the heights of success in his musical career, but also his greatest setbacks, in this city on the Danube.

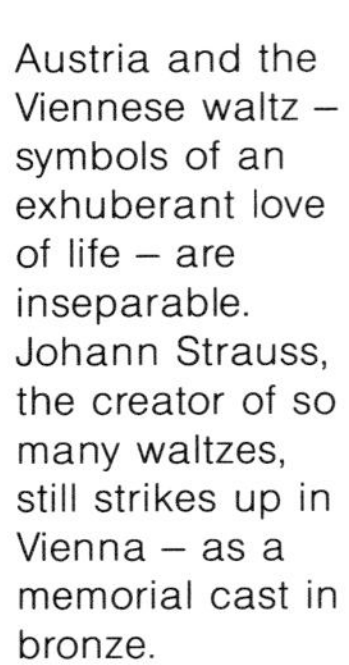

Austria and the Viennese waltz – symbols of an exuberant love of life – are inseparable. Johann Strauss, the creator of so many waltzes, still strikes up in Vienna – as a memorial cast in bronze.

A relict of bygone days: the Viennese Werkelmann, an organ-grinder who used to do the rounds of the backyards to play the people a tune or two.

The Donauturm ("Danube Television Tower") in the Danube Park is 827 feet high and the tallest structure in Vienna. In the foreground, the romantic moorings on the old arm of the Danube.

The whole world looks to this centre: the UNO City, inaugurated in 1979. In the foreground, the Danube, which is only really blue in the title of the waltz, . . .

Burgenland is still a "Land of Castles": 68 strongholds have been preserved. One famous fortress is the Lockenhaus, once a centre of chivalrous life. However, the name Erzsébeth Bàthory-Nadasdy, once lady of the castle, calls to mind one of the most atrocious sex killers to go down in history. The local monks reported that the piercing screams of her victims could be heard every night.

The records of the fortress of Schleining (left) show that it was only taken once in its 900 years of history. – The name of Joseph Haydn is inseparably bound up with Eisenstadt, the capital of Burgenland. He composed most of his symphonies here, and this was also where he was laid to rest. Below left: the Great Hall of the Esterházy Palace, known as the Haydn Hall. Below right: Forchtenstein. Every year plays by the Austrian dramatist Franz Grillparzer are performed in the dried-up moat of this castle.

The wine-growers of Rust are proud and self-confident. Once one has won them over, they are most hospitable. – Immense distances and boundless freedom with a touch of melancholy in splendid natural surroundings: all these are still to be had in Burgenland.

A thriving pottery industry has arisen at Stoob, a village in the centre of Burgenland: the Plutzer, a pot-bellied jug with a narrow neck is a typical product. – Burgenland: that means thatched roofs, storks, draw-wells (right), ponds, reeds, maize, idyllic villages and rows of long, low houses as in Mörbisch.

W